Luna Little Legs is a beautifully illustrated, skillfully designed book for young children who have experienced domestic violence, abuse and coercive control. An important feature of the text is that it has three different endings, so the book can be tailored to the life experience of children who are engaging with it. The Domestic Abuse Act 2021 recognises children as direct victims of domestic abuse, and *Luna Little Legs* is a perfect addition for professionals who are working with and supporting child victims – who, given the prevalence of domestic abuse, are likely to be present in every early years and childcare setting. The accompanying *Professional Guide* provides advice on how to use the book effectively, as well as signposting the reader to further tools.

You do not need to be an expert on domestic abuse to find the book valuable: the *Professional Guide* provides a wealth of information so that anyone can feel confident about using this wonderful resource.

Dr Emma Katz, PhD,
Senior Lecturer in Childhood and Youth,
Liverpool Hope University, UK.

Helping Young Children to Understand Domestic Abuse and Coercive Control

This guidebook is designed to support professionals with the effective use of the storybook, *Luna Little Legs*, which has been created to help preschool-aged children understand about domestic abuse and coercive control.

Sensitively and accessibly written, the guidebook presents the adult with comprehensive information regarding domestic abuse and coercive control, and its impact on young children, putting them in a position to have important and informed interactions with the young children in their care. These conversations help children to make sense of their experiences of domestic abuse, giving them the opportunity to vocalise their feelings and to understand what to do when something feels not right.

Key features of this book include:

- Page-by-page notes to support the sensitive reading of the *Luna Little Legs* story
- Accessible information about domestic abuse and coercive control based on the latest research
- A comprehensive list of helplines and organisations in place to support adult victims of domestic abuse.

This is an essential companion to the *Luna Little Legs* story, and is crucial reading for anybody working with young children and their families who are experiencing, or have experienced, domestic abuse and coercive control.

Catherine Lawler is a qualified specialist children's counsellor, trauma practitioner and a childhood survivor of domestic abuse. She has extensive experience of working with children, young people and families as well as developing and facilitating training on the issue of domestic abuse and coercive control. Catherine is co-author of *Domestic Violence and Children: A Handbook for Schools and Early Years* (Routledge, 2010) and *Floss and the Boss: Helping Children Learn About Domestic Abuse and Coercive Control* (Routledge, 2021).

Norma Howes has trained in social work, child forensic psychology and psychotherapy. She is also a trainer and consultant for workers from agencies dealing with all forms of trauma, abuse and neglect and their impact. She has a special interest in domestic abuse and sexual trauma. She has written guides for *Community Care Inform: A Trauma Model* for working with i) Domestic Abuse, ii) Sexual Exploitation, iii) Contact between Children and their Families, and a *Guide on the Neurobiological Impact of Contact*.

Nicky Armstrong, BA (Hons) Theatre Design, MA Slade School of Fine Arts, has illustrated 30 books which have been translated and published in seven countries. She has achieved major commissions in both mural and fine art painting.

Helping Young Children to Understand Domestic Abuse and Coercive Control

A Professional Guide

CATHERINE LAWLER AND NORMA HOWES
ILLUSTRATED BY NICKY ARMSTRONG

Routledge
Taylor & Francis Group

LONDON AND NEW YORK

Cover image: Nicky Armstrong

First published 2023
by Routledge
4 Park Square, Milton Park, Abingdon, Oxon OX14 4RN

and by Routledge
605 Third Avenue, New York, NY 10158

Routledge is an imprint of the Taylor & Francis Group, an informa business

British Library Cataloguing-in-Publication Data
A catalogue record for this book is available from the British Library

Library of Congress Cataloging-in-Publication Data
A catalog record has been requested for this book

ISBN: 978-1-032-07257-9 (pbk)
ISBN: 978-1-003-20617-0 (ebk)

DOI: 10.4324/9781003206170

Typeset in Antitled
by Apex CoVantage, LLC

Printed in the UK by Severn, Gloucester on responsibly sourced paper

Access the Support Material: www.routledge.com/9781032072579

This book is dedicated to my beautiful cat Isobel, the real Luna. She is my constant companion and a source of unconditional love. I had heard that many people become cat mums or dads more through accident than design and this was the case for me. The day Isobel rocked up to my house and refused to leave was a blessed day. She turned up out of the blue at a time in my life when I would soon desperately need her, I didn't know this, but she clearly did.

This book is also dedicated to the little people out there who live with the terror of domestic abuse, who attempt to navigate this every day and are finally seen as victims in their own right.

Catherine

Contents

1. Before you use this book

The experience of being read to can often feel nurturing for a child, and we hope that Luna's story will help children with similar experiences feel less alone. It is important to remember that young children are less likely to be able to tell us with words if they are experiencing discomfort or distress. We need to be mindful of any possible triggers for these feelings and how we notice and respond to them. Reading this *Professional Guide* will help you to recognise if, or when, these triggers happen.

Before reading the book to or with a child it is important to read the book through, out loud by and to yourself. Notice the tone of your own voice and any changes in it as you read the different pages; does it get quieter, louder, stutter, stick on any particular words or make you reluctant to turn the page? Notice any changes in your breathing. These changes could indicate you are becoming a bit dis-regulated and moving towards the edge of your window of tolerance. If this was to happen while you are reading the book to the child, the child would notice and may become dis-regulated in response to your response rather than the content of the book. This is not suggesting you should read the book in a monotone but to make sure you are already aware of your own potential wobbles. Reflect on and wonder about these, so that you can focus on noticing if the child is wobbling. By noticing this is happening to you when it starts means you are then able to re-regulate your own tone of voice – either up or down, faster or slower – depending on whether you or the child is heading towards hyper- or hypo-arousal. See Chapter 5 for information on the window of tolerance.

It is also important to think about the age and language skills of the child you are thinking of reading the book to. Think about what you know about their past or current experiences, and who, if anyone, might be annoyed with them or put at risk by the child chatting about the content of the book at home. It is useful to think of questions the child might ask you and also what answers you might need to give. These answers must never be a lie but just give reassurance rather than more worries. For example, if the child asks, 'What will happen to Luna?', it is useful to reply 'What would you like to happen to Luna?' While reading with the child be aware of any changes in the child's breathing and any tension in their body to see if the answers you give to any of their questions do reassure and help them relax.

Keep in mind that what works to reassure or help one child relax might frighten another, e.g. offering a few moments of quiet reflection, a hug or praise for being curious will work for one, but not for another where at home something nasty happens before or after it is quiet or after a hug or after a question has been asked.

Some things to try to help and teach a young child to re-regulate their arousal – slow down your own breathing and relax your body, offer a hug but never insist, play a game which needs movement but not running around, teach the child how to put their hands on opposite shoulders to give themselves a hug with gentle pats called butterfly kisses. See page 28 for some more ideas/suggestions.

Practising how to use the book will enable you to engage with a child confidently. A few more things to think about: where will the book be put after you have finished reading it, and how will you end the sessions you are undertaking? Your child might decide the book is just for him or her or want to choose where the book is kept. If the child's choice fits with what you think is best for the child, great; if not, think ahead to how you will resolve this difference. When using the book you may choose to just to explore particular sections rather than reading it in its entirety.

Domestic abuse and animals

Research has documented the correlation between domestic abuse, coercive control and the abuse of animals. Our pets often form part of our family unit offering companionship and unconditional love. For children experiencing domestic abuse and coercive control, their pets can take on even more significance. Pets may offer and/or have offered children emotional support and comfort, be soothing, therapeutic and provide a focal point to the day.

Think about snuggling into your cat or dogs' fur, feeling safe, loved and accepted in that moment. The hormone oxytocin is being released just thinking about this and will be released in larger doses when doing it. These small opportunities to relax and adjust are incredibly important for children who are stressed and lived in fear. Sometimes children will express more concern, love and care for their pet than they do for their siblings, parents or friends.

Perpetrators may have threatened to or have actually hurt pets to psychologically control and cause distress or for revenge and punishment. It will be useful before reading this book to a child to know if they have pets and if these pets have been mistreated or been left behind to prepare for, and enable you to think about, any triggers and how you will deal with them.

Please see the Website section (p. 34) at the end of this guide for details of pet fostering services for families fleeing domestic abuse.

2. Gender and parenting issues

The statistics on relational violence and coercive control consistently report a high percentage of perpetrators as male and their victims as female. The characters in this book are therefore based on these statistics. Due to the age range of children this book is written for, Little Luna's story describes the physical manifestations of domestic abuse, but we need to be mindful that these may typically exist in the context of or are underpinned by coercive control.

An issue which might come up is that unlike Little Luna's mum who shows Little Luna how much she loves her, notices her distress and takes action, the child you are reading the book with might not have had that experience. Experiencing domestic abuse and coercive control can disable or reduce the victim's ability to behave as Little Luna's mum does.

Key adults supporting the victim parent, statistically usually the mother

The story we have written includes a Mummy and Daddy. If you are able to, and it's appropriate, the characters' genders can be adapted. Because the victim parent is usually the mother, we continue to refer to her as "she". Domestic abuse has a detrimental impact on parenting. It can deprive the victim parent of the authority, confidence, physical and emotional strength to parent effectively. It can render her emotionally unavailable and make it difficult for her to play and interact positively with her children and put a strain on her relationships with her children. She may also find it difficult to impose boundaries on behaviour. A mother may need help but may feel so low and powerless that she does not seek it. The onus may therefore need to be on professionals to reach out to her. Key adults have an important role to play in getting to know and supporting the victim parent.

Supporting mothers can be fundamental to supporting children. Katz (2019) cites numerous studies that identify that warm, attuned, sensitive and responsive parenting from mothers tends to increase children's resilience and reduce the severity of the negative impacts that they experience. However, fear of repercussions from a partner can make it very difficult for some mothers to be open and express concerns or feelings. Staff should not interpret an apparent reluctance to engage as not caring, and labels such as 'hard to reach' can be unhelpful. The challenge is to build a trusting relationship and facilitate opportunities to talk.

Nurseries, mother and baby groups and schools are ideally placed to reach out to mothers in need of help. Mothers visit regularly, often without their partner. Drop-off and pick-up times may be a mother's best or only opportunity for a chat with someone outside the family who has picked up that something is amiss.

Developing a relationship may take time, commitment and sensitivity; trust is paramount. Bear in mind, some mothers may feel they need to keep authorities at a distance.

Some suggestions:

- Try to see the mother separately from her partner.
- Be open, providing a listening ear.
- Give her a private space and time to talk. It may help to ask open-ended, non-threatening questions, for example, 'How are things at home?'
- In the unlikely situation where you are asked not to tell anyone about what you are told, start by asking what the person is scared might happen if someone else were to know. This might be asked because of a threat; remember for a threat to work it will always have at least a grain of truth in it, or previously negative contact with authorities. Never say you will keep what you are told a secret. Work together to find a helpful way forward.
- Help parents and young children build better relationships through play. Highlight the importance of this.
- It may be appropriate to signpost mothers to organisations for women experiencing domestic abuse (see section on websites and helplines) as well as specialist parenting programmes.
- Think about how to provide information which is on a small piece of paper on a fringed edge and therefore easy to tear off /take away/hide or useful apps. Parents often wait in areas with noticeboards or leaflet racks. Posters and flyers can provide information about sources of support. They also give the message that the institution is aware of and taking a stand on the issue. However, please make sure these do not include confidential details of resources which would alert the perpetrator to who or where these are.

Over time, a mother may be more open to talking about her situation, the pressures on her and her concerns. Some practitioners working to gain a better understanding of a child affected by coercive control may feel in a position to ask children and mothers about the constraints that are placed on their movements, their activities and who they can engage with inside and outside the home. Practitioners could also talk to children and mothers about whether there are things that they do, or refrain from doing, because of the reactions of perpetrators/fathers, and how this might be affecting children (Katz 2016b).

Promoting, modelling and supporting positive play sessions with mothers and young children

Once a relationship of trust has been built with the mother, the key adult may be able to demonstrate and support play sessions with her and her child. This can be supportive of the mother and strengthen the parent-child relationship. By facilitating time and space with her child and modelling enjoyment of fun, shared play, such activities can help re-establish the emotional availability of the mother which may have been damaged or lessened by the behaviour of the perpetrator.

In the longer term, professionals may be in a position to support mothers and children to talk to each other about domestic abuse. Research has found that some children purposefully refrain from initiating discussions with their mother about domestic abuse, due to not wanting to upset or burden her (Mullender et al. 2002, Humphreys et al. 2006).

Contact

It is of paramount importance that whoever is engaging with a child regarding contact is someone with experience in dealing with the impact domestic abuse and coercive control have on children. Whoever this is needs to be aware of how difficult it is, if not impossible, for a child who has lived with someone who frightened them, did not give them a voice or an opinion but instead insisted on agreement and compliance, to independently express their wishes and feelings.

It is therefore very important that a great deal of care is taken to make sure that the way the interviewer behaves and asks questions does not give the wary or compliant child a clue what the interviewer wants. For all children, and especially for young children, their opinions and feelings will be seen in their behaviour before, during and after contact. It is very difficult for young children, indeed any child who has lived with domestic abuse and coercive control, whose thinking and verbal skills are not yet sophisticated enough to be able to express an opinion, especially when that opinion might lead to a disagreement with consequences for one person, some people or everyone.

3. The characters

Little Luna

Little Luna represents a child whose home environment is one of domestic abuse and coercive control. Her story portrays the typical thoughts, feelings, reactions and behaviours of a young child who is stressed, confused and scared. The story illustrates in rhyming couplets her possible journeys with three different endings: remaining at home, going to a refuge and on to a new home or back to the family home with Dad.

Little Luna's Mum

Little Luna's Mum represents a parent who is a victim of domestic abuse and coercive control. This story focuses on her attempts to reassure and comfort Little Luna during the different stages of their journey.

Little Luna's Dad

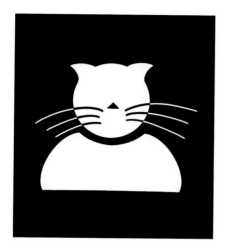

Little Luna's Dad is the perpetrator of domestic abuse and coercive control. There are no images of him in the story. However, his actions and behaviour are represented in the manifestation of the fear and uncertainty that Little Luna experiences.

Ringo, Cookie and Mittens

Ringo, Cookie and Mittens represent Little Luna's friends who are her best friends and very important to her.

Refuge worker

The refuge worker is the key adult who provides support and assistance to Little Luna and her mother whilst they are living in the refuge.

About the endings – why three alternatives with no finite ending?

We wondered when writing this book how to end Little Luna's story. Every child's lived experience will be unique and that's the reason we want you to choose how to end the book in a way that will fit with the actual or possible ending(s) of the child you are supporting. This will enable individual children to connect Little Luna's experiences with their own and, like her, be able to better understand and have words for their own feelings, confusions, losses and gains. And, indeed, hopes for the future.

4. Teacher/helper's notes

Page 2 Little Luna represents a well-nurtured child. She and her Mum love each other very much. Little Luna lives in a family where there is domestic abuse and coercive control. The perpetrator is her Dad.

Page 4 Little Luna enjoys nursery, where she has lots of friends, nurture, routines and fun.

All are foundations for a happy and healthy childhood.

Page 6 Little Luna and Mum trust and love each other. Mum responds to Little Luna's needs instinctively with care and predictability.

Pages 8–10 Little Luna is in bed hearing her Mum being hurt by her Dad. She cannot see what is happening but can hear and imagine it. Her responses are typical of a child experiencing pervasive fear and uncertainty. Tummy aches, wobbly legs, body stiffening, difficulty sleeping and regulating emotions, she may be in a high state of arousal.

Pages 12–14 Little Luna worries she may be responsible for her Dad hurting or arguing with her Mum. It is very usual for children (and adults) experiencing domestic abuse and coercive control to blame themselves when they are trying to make sense of something which they know is not alright. It is also common for a perpetrator to blame a child which reinforces this core belief, e.g. I tripped over your toys! Why do you look scared, silly kitten?

Here Little Luna's mum is acknowledging Little Luna's confusion and distress, and her emerging feelings of self-blame or "I'm bad." She tries to help Little Luna think of some strategies to use when she feels frightened or unsure.

Little Luna is experiencing a host of different emotions which mirror the ever-changing environment in which she lives. It's important to remember that some abusive environments may be peppered with alternating and frequently changing periods of calm and chaos, with oppressive rules and kind responses from the perpetrator. Mum's empathic attunement, consistent care-giving, cuddles and their reciprocal interactions are a protective factor for Little Luna in the short and long term.

Domestic abuse and coercive control are fear driven. Fear is one of the main reasons victim/survivors remain.

This page leads on to the first ending and reflects the reality of many children who continue to live in environments where domestic abuse and coercive control is omnipresent, and there is the potential for further abuse.

The End, Part 1

Page 18 Mum feels so unsafe and frightened for them both. She knows she and Little Luna need to hide and must leave their home immediately, leaving everything behind.

Page 20 Little Luna and Mum are now in the refuge where they are made welcome by staff and other cats and kittens who are there for the same reason. As well as feeling relief, moving into the refuge leaves Little Luna with feelings of uncertainty, loss (family, friends, possessions), lack of control and anxiety. It is important to remember that a child in a physical place of safety may not *feel* safe immediately, and this can take a long time to happen. Being on alert and vigilant takes a long time, and a lot of trust, to change.

Page 22 Mum and Little Luna are now settling in the new home. Many children will live in a refuge before moving to a new home. New homes can bring happiness but also a lot of challenges. These pages conclude the second ending and represent many children's realities.

The End, Part 2

Pages 26/28 Dad re-enters Little Luna's life. He promises violence will not happen again with demonstrations of changes in that behaviour, with apologies, gifts and smiles reinforcing the hope that the changes are happening and will continue to happen.

Returning home also reflects the reality of many children's lives.

The End, Part 3

5. Attachment and the "window of tolerance"

Infants and young children need at least one emotionally available parent/adult who consistently responds to their needs, for example being held, comforted, soothed, having their feelings acknowledged, put into words and understood. This is a very important part of making sure a child's development is on course. Children are born with an innate need for safety and attachment. Their brain, the right brain limbic system, enables attunement or connection with the Mum's right brain limbic system, communicating without words but with a cry, or facial and body movements, that something is needed.

The Mum's empathic attunement enables her to know what her baby needs, put words to these needs and, importantly, meet those needs before the baby becomes too distressed. Not being able to meet these needs is distressing for both baby and mother. Consistently and lovingly meeting these needs enables the Mum to begin to use purposeful, age-appropriate mis-attunement to enable her growing child to learn that behaviour has an impact on other people which hurts both the child and the other person. This is the beginning stage of the child learning about empathy. It is empathy which enables us to empathically attune to someone's feelings, notice how they are feeling *and* how we are feeling, then primarily meet the needs of the other putting our own needs second. Attunement without empathy results in noticing what someone else is feeling or needing but instead of meeting their needs manipulating and using their needs, to please and/ or be loved, to make them meet one's own needs first. This is often seen in the child, then later as an adult, being selfish, not able to share, easily angered and attention seeking.

Another important aspect of children's development is learning about how to manage and regulate their emotions and the feelings in their body. Children are not born with this knowledge and learn it through emotional interactions and playing games with parents, siblings, other adults and children. The adult notices when there is enough excitement and "externally" calms the child down until the child is able, in familiar situations at first then in unusual or new experiences, to notice this for themselves and begin to self-regulate or "internally" manage their arousal or excitement. For example, the adult playing boo stops when it is still fun and before it is distressing or makes the child cry. Playing boo, which is actually hiding from the child, starts off as interesting, exciting and challenging but it also increases their fear of loss and anxiety. Reappearing at the right moment, through empathic attunement, calms the child down and reassures the child the adult is still there. This and other games lead developmentally to object permanence, an important foundation for a secure attachment, and in an age-appropriate way children learn how to deal with separation and loss. That is, you don't have to actually see or touch something to know it exists, and separation from the adult is increasingly manageable. The "window of tolerance", which offers a way of thinking about how we function optimally, i.e. our own unique state of arousal, is widened.

Of course, no parent is perfect and mistakes are made. Making a mistake can be another way of "widening the window" as long as there is an immediate and heartfelt apology with explanation and care giving, reassurance and kind words to enable trust to be re-established and recovery to begin. See the Appendix for examples of this.

There are two coping outcome or answers, strategies or behaviours which are needed to deal with "out of the window" experiences: 1) hypo-arousal/shutting down, or 2) hyper-arousal/frantic responses or sometimes swinging between the two. These answers are often seen as the problem with little or no curiosity about what they might be the answer to. They can mimic the diagnostic criteria for ADD (attention deficit disorder), ADHD (attention deficit hyperactivity disorder), ASD (autistic spectrum disorder) or depression, dissociation, extreme tiredness and when both hyper and hypo are used a diagnosis of bipolar or borderline/unstable personality disorder. Usually when this happens the blaming/shaming question 'What is wrong with you?' is asked. It would be much more appropriate to ask 'What has happened to you?' or 'What is happening to you?' which does not blame or shame but offers empathic curiosity and support.

Treatment or interventions which only examine the answers and don't look for the problem(s) which require or required these answers will have limited or even no success. Only if the behaviour is threatening to self or others does it need immediate intervention. If not, it is the problem or trauma causing the "out of the window" behaviour which needs intervention.

All children will experience positive and tolerable stress with positive and tolerable results. The term "toxic stress" developed at the Harvard Centre and used by the 70/30 campaigning charity to replace the word "trauma", describes the physical impact on the body and the emotional brain when both are overloaded. Experiencing prolonged activation of the stress response system in the absence of protective relationships has a negative effect on the brain and the body (Felitti et al. 1998).

It is not unusual for one child in a family to be "stressed" by what is happening while another finds it traumatic and intolerable. The behaviour or coping strategies which follow are externalised or internalised. A child who internalises their distress can be positively described as resilient, a wrong assumption made that the child was less hurt by what was done, or what was missing, because that child's internalised behaviour does not suggest, draw attention to or indicate enough upset (Cairns 2002). The child who externalises their behaviour to draw attention to their level of hurt can be negatively viewed as being oppositional, difficult, attention seeking, manipulative and is referred for a diagnosis.

Resilience, adverse and benevolent childhood experiences

Bowlby (1951) noted that the securely attached child is more likely to approach the world with confidence. Erikson (1950) talked of basic trust, consistency, continuity and sameness of experience. Domestic abuse and coercive control by its very nature undermines this, reducing resilience, increasing the impact of adverse childhood experiences (ACEs) and the need for benevolent experiences to balance these negatives.

Children living in highly controlled and violent environments find home can be a stressful, unpredictable and frightening place. Many children feel they need to always be on guard in anticipation of something fearful happening and therefore live in a state of constant fear. This is likely to include a preoccupation not just with their own safety but also with their mother's, sibling's and pet's safety.

Being separated from someone you worry about, or who worries you, can make a child and an adult even more anxious and desperately want to know where they are, make sure they are all right, if they still present a threat or might have changed. This sort of anxiety creates what is called a trauma bond, part of a disorganised attachment, rather than a secure attachment (James 1994). A secure attachment makes developmentally appropriate separation manageable. A trauma bond, on the other hand, makes separation and missing intensely painful. Perhaps this is one way of explaining returning to visit or live with that person again.

Research in the USA (Felitti et al. 1998), followed by similar research in the UK, found that ACEs not only impacted on a child's psychological development but also their immune systems and physical health.

The impact of these negatives can be reduced by the child having experiences which will build their resilience. Research on what is helpful identifies one important factor which underpins and creates several others. This is the presence of a caring, nurturing adult who lets the child know the child is OK but what is happening at home is not. It is this that leads to an appropriate sense of humour, the ability to imagine and create positives out of negatives and make and sustain future relationships. Other factors include: enjoyment of school, experiencing teachers and adults who care, opportunities to have fun and enjoyable times, predictability and routines. While these are important to reduce the impact, the first priority is to provide services, interventions and relationships which stop or at least reduce the domestic abuse and coercive control.

6. How young children experience domestic abuse and coercive control

Definitions of domestic abuse and coercive and controlling behaviour

The Domestic Abuse Act 2021 creates a statutory definition of domestic abuse based on the existing cross government definition.

Abusive behaviour is defined in the Act as any of the following:

- Physical or sexual abuse
- Violent or threatening behaviour
- Controlling or coercive behaviour
- Economic abuse
- Psychological, emotional or other abuse.

For the definition to apply, both parties must be aged 16 or over and "personally connected".

"Personally connected" is defined in the Act as parties who:

- Are married to each other
- Are civil partners of each other
- Have agreed to marry one another (whether or not the agreement has been terminated)
- Have entered into a civil partnership agreement (whether or not the agreement has been terminated)
- Are or have been in an intimate personal relationship with each other
- Have, or there has been a time when they each have had, a parental relationship in relation to the same child
- Are relatives.

Controlling behaviour is:

designed to make a person subordinate and/or dependent by isolating them from sources of support, exploiting their resources and capacities for personal gain, depriving them of the means needed for independence, resistance and escape and regulating their everyday behaviour.

Coercive behaviour is: an act or a pattern of acts of assault, threats, humiliation and intimidation or other abuse that is used to harm, punish or frighten their victim.

(Home Office 2015).

Professionals should note that coercive or controlling behaviour in an intimate or family relationship became a criminal offence in 2015, as part of the Serious Crime Act 2015.

A list of coercive and controlling behaviours from the Home Office (2015) includes:

- Isolating a person from their friends and family
- Depriving them of their basic needs
- Monitoring their time
- Monitoring a person via online communication tools or using spyware
- Taking control over aspects of their everyday life, such as where they can go, who they can see, what they wear and when they can sleep
- Depriving them of access to support services, such as specialist support or medical services
- Repeatedly putting them down, such as telling them they are worthless
- Enforcing rules and activity which humiliate, degrade or dehumanise the victim
- Financial abuse including control of finances, such as only allowing a person a punitive allowance
- Threats to hurt or kill
- Threats to a child
- Criminal damage (such as destruction of household goods).

Under the Act, councils across England will have a legal duty to provide life-saving support such as therapy, advocacy and counselling in safe accommodation, including refuges. It also extends the controlling or coercive behaviour offence to cover post-separation abuse.

Professionals should note that the largest predictors of intimate partner homicide are emotionally abusive controlling relationships and victim instigated separation.

Prevalence

- There are some 2.3 million victims of domestic abuse a year aged 16–74 (two-thirds of whom are women) and more than one in ten of all offences recorded by the police are domestic abuse related (www.gov.uk)
- Thirty per cent of children or young people had tried to intervene to stop abuse (SafeLives 2017)
- Ninety-five per cent of children were often at home when the abuse took place (SafeLives 2017)
- Seventy-four per cent were a direct witness to the abuse (SafeLives 2017)
- Ten per cent were injured as the result of the abuse of a parent (SafeLives 2017).

Victims of coercive control have described home life as being like walking on eggshells: having to ask permission to do everyday things and living in constant fear of not being able to meet the abuser's demands. It involves extreme regulation of everyday life. Research also highlights how children are direct victims of coercive control. Research conducted by Katz (2016a) into the harm inflicted by coercive control describes how fathers/father-figures' behaviours entrapped children (and their mothers) in constrained situations where children's access to resilience building and developmentally helpful persons and activities was limited. The impacts of perpetrators/fathers preventing children from spending time with their mother, visiting grandparents or going to other children's houses may contribute to emotional and behavioural problems in children.

Katz (2016b) describes different ways in which a perpetrator may impose control on the family:

- Micro-managing day-to-day activity and choices
- Control of space, time and movement within the home, including the time the mother spends with her children and the rooms/space they can use; locking them in or out of the house; preventing the mother and children from leaving the house (Katz 2016a)
- Controlling and limiting their access to food. This can include imposing rules about what is eaten when, who eats first, who can touch the food in cupboards or in the fridge.

For children living with domestic abuse and in a highly controlled environment, home is stressful and unpredictable. Some children always feel on guard, living in a state of almost constant fear and high arousal. This may include preoccupation and worried about their mother's, siblings', pet's or own safety.

The Duluth Domestic Abuse Intervention Programs (2017)

Since the early 1980s, Duluth, a city in northern Minnesota, has been an innovator of ways to hold perpetrators accountable and keep victims safe.

The "Duluth Model" is an ever-evolving way of thinking about how a community works together to end domestic abuse. It provides useful diagrams, "wheels", showing the interlinked issues and various manifestations of power and control related to domestic abuse.

How living with domestic abuse and coercive and controlling behaviour affects young children

Often when we think of victims of domestic abuse we think of adult victims. More recently it has been acknowledged that children are victims in their own right. The new Domestic Abuse Act 2021 explicitly recognises children as victims if they see, hear or experience the effects of abuse.

Below are some examples of how of children are often victimised by the perpetrator as an extension of their controlling tactics.

Using intimidation

- Instilling fear in the child through gestures, looks, or noises
- Actual violence or threats of violence to the child's other family members, pets, and favourite toys
- Not allowing the child to have a voice, choice or opinion. Children may learn it is not safe to express their feelings (be seen but not heard)
- Being an ever-present threat resulting in the child being in a prolonged state of hypervigilance, perceiving danger everywhere.

Using emotional abuse

- Insulting, belittling and shaming the child
- Insulting and belittling the other parent to/in front of the child
- Using the child as a confidante; this may involve the child being treated favourably by the perpetrator who provides justifications for their abusive behaviour towards the other parent
- Using the child an accomplice; this may involve the child being coerced to be involved with the abuse, which can take many forms including refusing to respect the other parent's authority to actual physical and emotional abuse of the other parent
- Emotionally inconsistent parenting, rules and boundaries; a lack of predictability and security.

Using isolation

- Controlling where a child can go and who they can see
- Preventing a child from seeing family and friends
- Attempts to disrupt and undermine the child's relationship with the other parent
- Preventing access to the other parent, i.e. cuddles, one-to-one time, bedtime stories, fun and laughter
- Attempts to disrupt and undermine sibling relationships
- A child having to keep secrets which may cause them to feel helpless and hopeless.

Minimising, denying and blaming

- Perpetrator blaming the child and others for the abuse they are subjected to
- Perpetrator refusing to accept responsibility for their behaviour and actions
- Perpetrator insisting there's nothing wrong in the family
- Scapegoating the child; this may involve the children being blamed for tensions at home and whose behaviour is then used to justify violence.

Misusing or abusing adult privileges

- Treating the child like a servant
- The child experiencing overly harsh punishment, discipline, punitive rules and consequences
- Rigid modelling of gender roles to the child
- Bullying the child.

Using economic abuse

- Withholding money for the child's basic needs
- Using money to control or bribe the child
- Using the child as an economic bargaining tool in court proceedings
- Conditional control of or withholding child maintenance
- Withholding permission for or not allowing the child to have extracurricular activities.

Using coercion and threats

- Creating a climate of pervasive fear
- Threatening harm to the child, other parent, siblings, family, friends
- Threats to harm pets or favourite toys
- Threat to kill self
- Threatening not to love the child, i.e. conditional parenting.

7. The impact of domestic abuse and coercive control on young children

In pregnancy

For some women, domestic abuse begins or escalates during and after pregnancy.

Domestic abuse during pregnancy is associated with several negative health and mental health outcomes for the foetus, mother and infant. It increases the risk of miscarriage, infection, premature birth, low birth weight, foetal injury and foetal death (Refuge website 2020). One study found that 15 per cent of women were assaulted in the first four months of pregnancy (For Baby's Sake 2021).

Domestic abuse and coercive control during and after pregnancy can have other significant implications for children, which may include:

- Severely raised levels of the stress hormone cortisol in the mother which can have a toxic effect on forming and new brain cells
- A larger and more sensitive amygdala and smaller than average hippocampus. The amygdala is the brain's "smoke detector" which when enlarged has increased sensitivity to anything which might indicate danger. The role of the hippocampus is not just to make sense of input from the senses but is also responsible for developing spatial and time awareness, short-term memory, organising and sequencing. This looks as if child is more clumsy/dyspraxic, fine motor skills are not as they should be, and playing games in turn is difficult, as is following rules
- Mother experiencing perinatal depression, from beginning of pregnancy till one year after the birth, preventing her availability to the child and attachment promoting behaviours
- Father's preoccupation with his own needs, preventing him expressing attachment-promoting behaviours
- Lack of stimulation. A mother who is anxious and depressed is much less likely to interact verbally and provide fun and stimulating play activities for her pre-school infant at a time that is crucial for language and cognitive development. A lack of environmental stimulation can lead to language deficits (McLaughlin, Sheridan and Lambert 2014) because this impacts on the growth of the parts of the brain necessary for receptive and expressive language making them smaller than average. Living with intolerable fear and terror switches off these parts of the brain resulting in the phrase "speechless with terror".
- The child's early abilities to make relationships being impacted by terror, fear, inconsistent care and rejection

- Language delay and difficulty. A home atmosphere of fear and unpredictability is not conducive to imitating and trying out new sounds and words. Babies and young children learn it is safer to be still and quiet and can then be, mistakenly, described as good babies (Barraclough 2005)
- Risk of child being injured whilst held by their mother
- Threats or hurt to the child to intentionally control, terrify and punish the mother
- All forms of abuse and neglect.

Pregnancy and early parenthood are opportune times for professional intervention. At these times women are more likely to have contact with health and other professionals such as early years settings.

However, there are several reasons why women may be reluctant to seek help; these include:

- Feeling ashamed (37 per cent)
- Worrying about experiencing more abuse as a consequence (33 per cent)
- Not knowing how to talk about the situation (33 per cent)
- Not thinking the situation is serious enough to seek help (32 per cent)
- Worrying about the consequences to their baby, in terms of action by the authorities (27 per cent)
- Not wanting to be judged (27 per cent) (For Baby's Sake 2021).

All of these reasons are explanations that are often mistaken for excuses. These explanations explain what makes it impossible for women to leave the perpetrator. Instead of asking a question with the word why, which is not at all helpful, it is better to ask questions starting with the word what. For example, "Why did you not leave?" needs to be changed to "What did you think would happen if you left?" or "What was it stopped you from leaving?"; "Why did you go back?" should be changed to "What was it that made you go back?" Asking questions starting with the word why makes victims, women and children feel victimised or diminished. Starting a conversation with why questions is blaming and shaming and also confirms feelings of self-blame, reinforcing what she has been told by the perpetrator.

In young children

It is important to remember that young children experiencing domestic abuse and coercive control are not a footnote to their parent's experiences. They are extremely sensitive to their surroundings, especially the emotional signals and states of their parents.

Young children experiencing domestic abuse and coercive control often find growing up difficult and may behave like a much younger child. This difficulty can be seen in any of the following:

- Regulating their emotions, managing feelings and behaviour
- Having reciprocal fun, interaction or laughter

- Asking for help
- Accepting praise
- Refusal to follow instructions by saying 'No!' or 'Won't'. Often children who live in highly controlled homes will attempt to gain some control of their external environment by engaging in power struggles, mimicking the perpetrator. This sometimes comes out in the form of bullying or being bullied and being described as controlling, oppositional or defiant.
- Exaggerated startle responses that can be followed by outbursts usually indicating unbearable levels of tension in the child
- Oversensitivity to sounds, smells and touch. This may also include eye contact from adults in case it is hostile or angry.
- Lack of attention and concentration. Another source of difficulties with concentration is their preoccupation with and worries about the safety of their mothers, siblings and pets at home.
- Hyper-alert and vigilant. Because they are on their guard they may continually be scanning and be distracted from their play. This can also cause fatigue and sleep difficulties.
- Excessive fear. This can make a child less able to engage with play activities and learning, concentrate, take in new information and reduce exploration narrowing their window of tolerance. This impacts heavily on their own learning and that of others.
- Mistrust of or clinging to adults. Some children may crave adult attention and behave in a way to get it – negative attention being better than no attention. These children can be very wearing for staff and sadly are often negatively called *attention* seeking rather than this behaviour being seen as *attachment* or *safe contact* seeking. Their behaviour impacts heavily on their own learning and that of others.
- Perceiving needing to keep the ordinary rules needed in nursery or school as confirmation that they are bad or not good enough and teachers as not liking them and being deliberately horrible.
- Friendships and social interactions. Children who have seen that making threats and shouting are effective means of exerting control and getting their own way repeat this behaviour within their play, in nursery and with friends.

Any or all of these issues can prevent a child from thriving in nursery and school. They cause distress, anxiety and affect their education in many ways. Each child's set of circumstances is unique, but different studies indicate that children living with severe or prolonged abuse are more likely to develop challenging behaviour and have significant social, emotional and mental health needs. They are more likely than others to find learning demanding and challenging.

Earlier research by Katz (2016a and b) outlines how children living with coercive control may have limited opportunities for self-determination. This can lead to them not feeling feel free to make choices, express ideas and develop a sense of independence and competence. In the nursery or classroom, we may see a child struggling to make choices about what they do, engage with the full range of play and learning activities, place themselves outside their comfort zone, challenge themselves, take risks or ask for help.

The psychological impact on children who live in fear

Children living with domestic abuse and coercive control may live with high and sometimes unbearable levels of fear and insecurity. Some may feel under almost constant threat. They may be challenging when getting ready for nursery or school and use delaying tactics such as running away or wetting themselves. They may be excessively clingy and stressed on arrival at nursery or school, finding it very difficult to separate from their mothers.

Some children may be so anxious they feel ill (for example, nervous tummy aches) during the day and worry about what will happen when they get home. Yet it is easy for the anxiety to go unrecognised in nursery or school. Children are then told off for being attention seeking instead of this being another example of affection or comfort seeking.

Younger children generally do not have the ability to express their feelings verbally so they communicate through their behaviour. It is useful to think of any behaviour as the child's, or even the adult's, answer to a problem rather than that the behaviour is the problem, e.g. wetting or soiling, licking lips, exaggerating or ignoring an injury, using violence to solve an argument or dispute.

The impact on personal emotional and social development

A framework for understanding the impact on personal emotional and social development (PSED) is broken down into three aspects in Early Years Matters (2019). These are: 1) self-confidence and self-awareness, 2) managing feelings and behaviour and 3) making relationships. This is useful when assessing the impact of domestic abuse and coercive control on the wholistic development of young children and whether or not they are meeting their milestones.

When there seems to be no impact at all

It is not possible for there to be no impact at all when a child is living with domestic abuse or coercive control. What has been written about already are the many obvious, unmissable behaviours which are seen when a child is externalising the impact. Some children may also have witnessed or found out for themselves that it is not safe to let anyone know they are distressed and terrified. It is safer to look smiley and happy and behave in a way that pleases. They will often appear not to notice or pay attention to anything unusual that happens when other children are immediately curious and alert. Internalising their distress in this way is shown in the research to have negative long-term physical, emotional and psychological consequences and must not be overlooked or ignored. Building trust with even just one predictable, safe, nurturing adult, even if it is only for a short amount of time, will sow the seeds of resilience and be a building block for future wellbeing.

8. Talking and listening to children to support safety planning

Recent research highlights the importance of talking directly to children about their capacity to cope in situations of domestic abuse (Callaghan et al. 2018). As important, or maybe more important, than talking to children is listening to them. This means when you are introducing yourself to a child instead of saying "I'm someone who talks to children", it's better to say "I'm someone who listens to children", or "I'm someone who talks to children but I'm also someone who loves listening to what they have to say".

The Luna story creates opportunities for adults to do this by exploring fearful and anxious feelings related to home and family life. Children can be helped to use and experiment with language relating to feelings. The Luna story can support some children to make sense of how they are feeling and what they are thinking. More broadly, it should help *all* children explore the concept of fear, safety and what they and others can do if they do not feel safe or well looked after. All children need to know that not just what they say will be important and heard but notice will also be taken of how they say it and thought will be given to what they might be meaning. The following key underlying messages should be conveyed:

- Their safety and wellbeing are important; adults should keep them safe
- Their thoughts and feelings matter
- If they feel fearful, they should seek help
- There are adults outside the home who can be trusted
- These adults may be able to help them, even in a situation that seems very difficult, for example, they have been told there is no one who will listen and threats have been used to stop them seeking help
- They can be helped to enjoy nursery and have fun.

When any child mentions a threat has been used to keep them silent, for this threat to work it has to have an element of truth in it or it won't work. Don't just dismiss the threat as nonsense, unlikely or not true but explore with the child what might be making the children believe it is true. For example, the child who says, "I was told my Mummy would leave me", or "I was told my Mummy would not love me anymore", or "If you tell someone will be hurt" must be fearful it is possible that these things would happen. Another common threat is "There's no point in telling anyone, no one will believe you because you tell lies". Perhaps Mummy has threatened to leave, or has left and returned, or the perpetrator has influenced the loving relationship between mother and child, or at some point the child has told a lie to stay safe or has witnessed someone being hurt.

Key questions and discussion points about feelings

- How does Luna show she is happy/sad/scared/angry?
- How does Luna's body show us she is feeling happy/sad/scared/angry?
- What is Luna's face telling us?
- Where in her body would she feel the wobbles? What would they feel like?
- Who could she talk to about her wobbly feelings?
- What makes Luna think that the difficult things at home were her fault?
- What helped Luna to feel safer and better?
- I wonder how Luna feels about going home?

Using the story to support children's thinking about safety in the home

The story can be used to talk with and listen to children, especially young children, about physical and emotional safety and to identify ways of keeping safe in the home. Questions might include:

- Where could Luna go to in her house if arguing and scary noises are happening?

    Luna might move away, for example, to another room, or go under the table, or crawl under her duvet.

- What could Luna do whilst she is in the other room?

    Encourage the children to think about things that can distract or comfort Luna.

- Who could Luna go to if she has wobbly feelings?

    Encourage children to identify who Luna might feel safe with or who might be helpful. Mum? Ringo, Cookie or Mittens? Be creative, for example, make a safety map/helpers' map. See Appendix, Luna's Paw. Use the paw prints or sticky notes to identify safe people/places.

- Who could children go to if they had these feelings?

    This is an opportunity to talk about other adults who might help; for example, family support workers, social workers, community police officers.

- If Luna has big feelings inside her head and body that don't feel good, what can help?

    Talk about fun activities, relaxation and mindfulness techniques.

- What could we say to Luna if she says it was her fault this happens?

    It's important not to start by saying it is not her fault but to explore with the child what makes Luna believe this. Sometimes children can tell when something nasty is going to happen and because waiting for it to happen can be very, very frightening the child does something as a diversion to make it happen or stop it happening. For example, drop a cup, argue, have a tantrum or tell a joke. This conversation hopefully will end with the children knowing it was not her fault or sow the seeds of future belief or wondering about whose fault it was (Howes 2009).

- What could have been said to Luna to make her feel safe?

     Listen to what words the child uses. These might be repeating words the child has heard the perpetrator say.

- What could we say or do to make Luna feel cared about?

     It might be appropriate to explain that it is not a child's fault if the adults argue. It also enables the child to provide kind words and positive affirmations to Luna.

Finally, after discussing the above, summarise what has been suggested. Go back to the start of the story and pull out the main themes, i.e. Luna's safe place, who Luna's helpers are.

Positive relationships – an antidote to trauma

"My aim is to collaborate with children to access their imagination, knowledge, and resources in order to create a safer family environment for the child, where the child is not a passive victim but has agency within his/her situation" (Castelino 2009).

Much research highlights the significance of positive interactions as potential buffers to the impact of childhood trauma and to help young children know that what is happening in their home is not OK, but they are OK. Professionals who see a child very regularly, for example, a teacher, teaching assistant, family support worker or learning mentor, are in prime position to offer practical and helpful support. Trusting relationships with familiar, key adults can be of great importance to children with a challenging home life. Adults close to the child can:

- Nurture a vulnerable child, give them a boost, provide additional pastoral care
- Listen and help a child with their thinking and understanding
- Provide helpful play activities
- Monitor wellbeing and notice changes in mood
- Liaise closely with the victim parent and refer on to other supporting agencies.

The French philosopher Montaigne (1533–1592) wrote, "It should be noted that children at play are not playing about. Their games should be seen as their most serious-minded activity". Maybe in the 21st century we can take his advice seriously.

The key adult role

Children living in homes with domestic abuse and coercive control may not have had the opportunity to internalise a sense of safety, security and trust in adults. Developing a trusting relationship with a supportive adult in nursery/school may take time, though a child may take the initiative and turn to an adult out of the blue.

The qualities of an effective key adult include the ability to be:

- Calm, confident, empathetic and a good listener
- Patient and persistent
- Fun-loving
- Reliable and consistent in their responses
- Proactive; good at networking within and beyond nursery
- Empathetic and trauma informed.

This role will work best when it is embedded in a positive nursery ethos. Effective supervision is essential. This means having time allocated on a regular basis with another adult/mentor/supervisor and with other professionals for case consultation. A key adult should feel supported and able to refer on, or signpost the parent, as appropriate.

Building a relationship, developing rapport

Kind, understanding, warm and empathetic relationships have a hugely positive impact. Vulnerable children will particularly benefit from adults who:

- Can provide a sensitive response to separation anxiety
- Are aware of a child's physical care needs; some children may arrive at nursery/school tired, hungry and thirsty; snacks and a drink are nurturing
- Understand attachment and its relevance to children who need warmth and care from one or two key adults
- Can nurture the child and communicate that they are unique and valued; can provide a secure base and a predictable routine; where possible the same room, same start time, same snack on offer
- Can provide soothing sensory experiences; opportunities for peace, quiet and relaxation
- Can encourage the child to recognise and express feelings
- Can help the child explore the concept of safety.

It is well documented that a constant state of chronic fear and associated stress has serious impacts on children's physical and mental health. Helping adults should be skilled in active listening and empathic communication. Secure and trusting relationships are a good antidote to relational trauma. PACE is a useful way to achieve this. It was developed by Dr Dan Hughes, an American psychologist who works with traumatised children. PACE stands for Playfulness, Acceptance, Curiosity and Empathy. These principles seem particularly appropriate as a framework to communicate with children who are experiencing, or have experienced, domestic abuse and coercive control to help promote the experience of safe relationships.

Playfulness

The purpose of playfulness is to enjoy being together in an unconditional way. Remembering that children who experience domestic abuse will often live in households where there are many constraints, conditions and consequences. Playfulness conveys approachability and nurture. The child can make mistakes, but the relationship remains intact. There is no shame or judgement.

Acceptance

Unconditional acceptance is fundamental to a child's sense of safety. It shows that there can be connection with their feelings without judgement. If children express distressing emotions about themselves or others, for example, "Nobody loves me", "I'm stupid", "I'm bad", they may be expressing a core belief about themselves. These beliefs are the most difficult to challenge in a way that makes the child feel understood. It would be easy for you to say, "You're not bad", but that will not often help the child. Instead, it is important to first of all accept these feelings, acknowledge and explore them using curiosity and empathy, for example, "I wonder where that thought came from" or "Has anyone told you that?" Then listen to their answer and continue being curious with acceptance and empathy.

Curiosity

It's important to be curious about the child's thoughts, feelings, wishes and intentions. Showing the child that you are interested in what is going on in their world and that you are willing to do something about it is powerful. Remember to avoid asking "Why?" It might be useful to try saying:

- Is it OK if I share my idea about what is going on for you?
- I might be wrong, but these are my ideas . . .
- I wonder what . . .
- I notice that . . .
- It sounds like . . .
- It feels like . . .
- I'm curious . . .
- I'm interested . . .

You could end your conversation by showing your appreciation that the child has trusted you by saying, "Thank you for letting me know, that can't have been easy for you".

Empathy

When you show empathy, you are showing the child that their feelings are important and valid to you, and that you are alongside them in their difficulty. You are showing that you can be with them, can put aside your own feelings and are trying hard to understand their feelings before you give advice or instructions.

One of the important benefits of using PACE is that this way of connecting with a child can help build resilience and this will widen their window of tolerance. Research done on what builds resilience in children consistently finds two important factors: 1) that the child met someone or found someone who made them feel loved, cared for and special, and 2) that someone gave them the message that it was what was happening in their life that was not OK, but they were OK. This little seed of empathy was able to grow when it was safe for it to grow resulting in resilience.

Approaches to helping children soothe and self-regulate

The 'calming' corner: Stressful home incidents can leave children overwhelmed and dysregulated, so provide a safe space for retreat; teach the child calming strategies and provide a calming kit. This may include a safe blanket or weighted blanket, sensory and soft toys and soothing music. Even young children may need help to communicate they need their safe space, so pre-agree a word, gesture or provide an expression card. The adults around the child must of course be aware of any signs the child will use to indicate help is needed.

Mindfulness activities: Can be helpful. Traumatised and frightened children are often in a heightened state of arousal and can perceive the simplest of situations as threatening. Mindfulness techniques can help minds and bodies to calm.

Butterfly hugs: The butterfly hug can sooth and focus children when they are experiencing strong emotions. The key adult can demonstrate to the child how to cross their arms, pat their back and be aware of their breathing. You can also count the pats starting quickly and gently slowing down until calm is achieved, visualise a butterfly flapping its wings and describe the butterfly.

Breathing bubbles: Most children love bubbles. As well as providing mutual enjoyment, bubbles can enable children to control their breathing and relax especially when the adult demonstrates how to do this.

After doing bubble popping, ask the child to blow only one big bubble. The adult teaches the child to take deep breaths from the stomach then slowly exhale.

Hand breathing/ Luna's Paw: Ask the child to draw around their hand, or the outline of Luna's paw, breathing in when drawing up the base on the thumb and fingers and breathing out when drawing back down from the tips of fingers. See Appendix for a copy of Luna's paw.

With some children it may be possible to explain that if they begin to feel angry or anxious and breathe deeply in the same way, it should help them calm down rather than do angry actions. Remember feeling angry is the answer to a problem and that what is done with that feeling or the child is told to do can be or cause an additional problem. What might be making the child feel angry? It is not unusual for someone, adult or child, to feel angry when they feel stupid, useless, helpless, hopeless, alone, betrayed.

Positive Paw: It is important for a child to be able to think about and talk about positive feelings and memories. Luna's paw could be used to draw positive memories, things that a child likes/enjoys doing/gains praise for or makes them smile. (See Appendix.)

Using technology for relaxation: Free apps such as *Chill Panda* and *Sesame Street Breathe* can help little brains and bodies calm down.

Sensory soothing toys/bags: With sensory toys such as playdoh, aroma dough, slime, fidget toys, the rhythmic movements can help anxious children calm down; joint activities help with rapport building.

Cuddle buddies: Cuddly toys can help children self-soothe and can also be used to help them think about the concept of safety: "Where could Teddy go if something was making him/her not feel safe?", "What could Teddy do if he/she didn't feel safe?", "How might Teddy feel?", "Who could help Teddy feel safe?"

The activities below can emphasise eye contact, touch, physical closeness, rhythmic movements and mutual enjoyment. Remember one of the goals is to help young children know that not all adults are scary or need to be in control.

Singing/Action rhymes: Ones that involve touch include "Row the Boat", "Round and Round the Garden", "Rock-a-Bye Baby".

Physical activities: Kicking a ball, jumping jacks, hopping, skipping, running, banging a drum, throwing bean bags, trampolining and relaxation exercises, these can all help children calm down and will release endorphins that trigger positive feelings. Yoga balls can be helpful to roll and relax on.

Art and craft activities: Painting, finger painting, playing with cornflour mixed with water, making a collage and card-making appeal to many children and provide opportunities for self-expression. Children may find messy activities very difficult especially when these have been discouraged in homes where there is a high level of control.

Dual drawing: The supporting adult begins drawing a picture, the child takes over by drawing the next bit and drawing the picture continues to alternate between the child and adult.

Bilateral scribbling to soft music: The child chooses two crayons one to hold in each hand and scribbles on paper to the beat of the music.

Puppy love/pet power: Sometimes schools have pets. Stroking animals can be soothing for stressed or anxious children. They encourage playfulness and produce an automatic relaxation response. Realistic cat and dog toys can be purchased that mimic animals breathing calmly, these can be useful to take with you into sessions.

Puppets, doll's house and small world toys and role play: These can help children express and explore feelings. Difficult situations can be acted out and the child can project their thoughts on to the puppets or toys. This can enable the adult to gain insight into the child's world. (Note that although many older children will play imaginatively and act out fantasies young children seldom do but will repeat what they say and hear. Beware of placing adult interpretations on the child's observations or language.)

Create a child's own relaxation backpack or calming case: An individual relaxation backpack /box can contain the resources the child chooses to help them feel calm, safe and regulated.

Safety planning with individuals

When it is known that children are living with domestic abuse and coercive control, safety planning is of paramount importance and will often be done in collaboration with the victim parent and other agencies.

The Luna story can be a helpful and non-threatening way to introduce a child to safety planning, initially by thinking about the options Luna and her mum had to stay safe. This might then lead to discussion about a child's own situation.

In the previous section, questions have been suggested to help a child think what Luna might do if there was an unsafe situation. When working one-to-one with a child, at the top of the age range for this book, these ideas might lead on to encouraging them to reflect on their own situation:

Please tell me or draw for me where you might go in your home? Draw yourself in your safe space, feeling safe.

What could you do while you are there? What would you do? Could you hold your cuddly toy tight, talk to it, sing a song to it, breathe calm feelings into your tummy?

Where would you go to if you have wobbly feelings? A little person might not be able to draw the people needed and you might need to do this for them. Ask the child what colour to use for each person.

If you have big feelings inside your head and body that don't feel good, what can you do? (Talk about some of the relaxation techniques you have introduced). What can I do to make you feel better?

Using the paw prints or sticky notes to identify safe people/places

The purpose of this is to help the child and you identify who are the safe people and safe places for this particular child. This should be done in a playful way as if it is a game, albeit a serious game with an important purpose. The person the child chooses may surprise you – that is their choice and only if you know this is not a safe person would you gently disagree with their choice. The child might not choose the person or people you would expect them to. Again, that is their choice. Without blaming or shaming the child for their choice, have a conversation about what made them choose that person.

Again, it is important you don't start with the word why. These questions blame and shame and will probably get the answer, " I don't know", silence or compliance and a search for the answer you wanted/looked for rather than what the child believes or thinks. Any question starting with why can instead be started with "Tell me what . . .", "Describe to me what . . ." or "Explain to me what . . .". Doing this opens the conversation up rather than closing it down, enabling you to listen to and explore with the child who is a safe person or where is a safe place. It is not unusual for a child to want to stick the note for someone frightening on the back of the paper or even outside the room door and then shut the door on the note. Again, that is their choice.

The paw prints can be copied onto a sheet of paper. You can also cut them out and use them as if they were sticky notes as well. You will know the child you are going to do this with and how to word your questions to give the child the most help. Write their answer, draw a picture or stick a sticky note to represent that person on each of the "toes".

Children love playing with sticky notes. There are so many different notes available now with characters of all sorts and colours as well as the standard square, circular or rectangular shapes. There are two different ways to do this: one involves using the characters the child lives with or, if that would be too upsetting, using the characters in the Luna story. The description which follows is for version one and is actually the same for version two but with the different characters.

Explain to the child the reason you are asking them to do this "game". This description will need to be in age-appropriate language to make it work and achieve the outcome needed. For example: "I would like you to do something with me so that I can see who lives in your home and how everyone gets on with each other." It is useful to ask the child to add who is their very, very best friend and who is their least liked person or worst enemy (using language the child will connect with) and then to place the sticky note for that person close or far away from their own note. This is a useful way to give the child a measure against which to place the notes for the other people. Using the sticky notes allows changes to be made as to where notes are placed. The sticky notes are particularly useful because of their stickiness. This stickiness can represent the stickiness of the relationships in a way using buttons or little dolls cannot.

Then ask the child to choose a note for themselves and after that for each person in their home/family, including pets. Either you or the child writes each person's name on their note, and these are put on a separate piece of paper in random places.

Depending on the age and competencies of the child, this exercise can be done several times to represent how relationships are at home whilst still living there, how they are today if the child is now not living at home and how the child would really, really like it to be.

The notes can also be used but instead of being about people to identify safe places and not safe places.

Paw patrol

If a child is going to or has moved to a refuge or a new place it is likely there will be questions or observations or different feelings which could be written on Luna's paw along with who might be able to offer some help or a solution, for example, "What might Luna want to know about the refuge?", "What could Luna tell us about living in the refuge?", "I wonder what Luna was thinking or feeling when she moved to her new home?", "I wonder who Luna would have been missing when . . .?"

Having thought about Luna the child will usually be able to share their own thoughts and feelings. See "The Hide Out", which houses many resources that can be used with children who are experiencing domestic abuse and have moved into a refuge.

Luna's Paw can be used to explore with a child who is important to them and who they would choose to go to if they were struggling with little, big or any sized feelings. It can also be used to explore who a child might have had to say goodbye to, what has been lost or left behind.

Helpful books for young children

Can't You Sleep Little Bear? (M. Waddell (1988) Walker Books)

A story about a child who has difficulty getting to sleep but does so with the help of Little Bear.

Floss and the Boss, Story Book and Professional Guide (C. Lawler and A. Sterne (2021) Routledge)

This book is designed to support professionals with the sensitive and effective use of the storybook, *Floss and the Boss*, created to help young children understand domestic abuse and coercive control. *Floss and the Boss* is for primary-aged schoolchildren and can be used with both individual children and in groups. *Luna Little Legs* is the companion book and has been created for younger children. It is to be used one-on-one with children by professionals.

Guess How Much I Love You (S. McBratney (1994) Walker Books)

A story about a baby rabbit who is very reassured by how much it is loved.

Misery Moo (J. Willis and T. Ross (2003) Henry Holt)

A book about trust and relationships; how friendship can weather anything. Somebody feels miserable and someone else keeps trying to cheer them up. This is relevant to how a child living with domestic abuse might feel; for example, Christmas being difficult. Children end up laughing.

No Matter What (D. Gliori (1999) Bloomsbury Magazine)

A story about a grumpy little fox who needs reassurance he will be loved 'no matter what' his feelings or behaviours.

Talking to My Mum. A Picture Workbook for Workers, Mothers and Children Affected by Domestic Abuse (C. Humphreys et al. (2006) Jessica Kingsley)

This book is a useful resource especially when for engaging children and their mothers in conversation about domestic abuse. It features illustrated activities with animal characters. Themes include: exploration of a range of memories and feelings, including changes in the family's living arrangements, talking about their father or happy times with siblings and friends.

The Huge Bag of Worries (V. Ironside and F. Rodgers (1996) Hodder Wayland)

A delightful story which can promote a discussion about fears, insecurity and worries for young children, encouraging children to find someone who will listen to them. The child feels much better when she has shared her worries with an adult.

Where the Wild Things Are (M. Sendak (1963) Harper and Row)

A children's classic. Max has adventures when he is sent to bed with no meal and sails away to a land of monsters. The illustrations contain a wonderful range of facial expressions that could stimulate discussion about different feelings and their underlying causes.

9. Websites and helplines

The Duluth Model is an ever-evolving way of thinking about how a community works together to end domestic violence.

www.theduluthmodel.org

0808 2000 247

For Babies Sake's vison is to empower parents to break cycles of abuse, to transform the life chances of families and move forward with positive change starting with the baby.

www.forbabyssake.org.uk

01438 873420

Galop run the national lesbian, gay, bisexual and trans domestic violence helpline.

www.galop.org.uk

0800 999 5428

Men's Advice Line is a charity that offers help and support for male victims of domestic violence. They run a men's helpline.

www.mensadviceline.org.uk

0808 901 0327

National Association for People Abused in Childhood (NAPAC) offers support to adult survivors of all types of childhood abuse, including physical, sexual, emotional abuse or neglect.

https://napac.org.uk

0808 801 0331

NSPCC is the UK's leading children's charity, preventing abuse and helping those affected to recover.

www.nspcc.org.uk

0808 800 5000

Paws Protect is a cat protection fostering service for families fleeing domestic abuse.

www.cats.org.uk/what-we-do/paws-protect

0345 2601 280

Rape Crisis is an organisation that offers support and counselling for those affected by rape and sexual abuse.

www.rapecrisis.org.uk

0808 802 9999

Refuge supports women and children who experience all forms of violence and abuse, including domestic violence, sexual violence, female genital mutilation, forced marriage, so-called honour-based violence, and human trafficking and modern slavery. Confidential domestic abuse helpline.

www.refuge.org.uk/get-help-now

0808 2000 247

Respect has a confidential helpline offering advice, information and support to help individuals to stop being violent and abusive to their partner.

www.respectphoneline.org.uk

0808 802 4040

RSPCA is the largest animal welfare charity operating in England and Wales. It has a 24-hour cruelty line to report cruelty, neglect or an animal in distress.

www.rspca.org.uk

0300 1234 999

Shelter helps people with housing needs by providing expert advice and support; they also run a national helpline.

https://england.shelter.org.uk

0808 800 4444

The Dogs Trust: The Freedom Project is a dog pet fostering service for families fleeing domestic abuse.

www.dogstrust.org.uk/help-advice/hope-project-freedom-project/freedom-project

0207 837 0006

Women's Aid is a charity that aims to end domestic violence/abuse against women and children. It provides a wide range of services and runs a national 24-hour, 7-days-a-week, confidential domestic abuse helpline.

www.womensaid.org.uk

0808 2000 247

Bibliography

Barraclough, N. E., Xiao, D., Baker, C. I., Oram, M. W. and Perrett, D. I. (2005) "Integration of Visual and Auditory Information by Superior Temporal Sulcus Neurons Responsive to the Sight of Actions", *Journal of Cognitive Neuroscience*. 17, pp. 377–391.

Bowlby, J. (1952) *Maternal Care and Mental Health,* 2nd ed. New York: World Health Organization.

Cairns, K. (2002) *Attachment, Trauma and Resilience*, London: BAAF.

Callaghan, J. E. M., Alexander, J. H., Sixsmith, J. and Fellin, L. C. (2018) "Beyond 'Witnessing': Children's Experiences of Coercive Control in Domestic Violence and Abuse", *Journal of Interpersonal Violence*, 33(10), pp. 1551–1581. doi: 10.1177/0886260515618946

Castelino, T. (2009) "Making Children's Safety and Wellbeing Matter", *Australian Social Work*, 62(1), pp. 61–73. doi: 10.1080/03124070802430726

Early Years Matters (2019) "Personal, Social and Emotional Development". Available online: www.early yearsmatters.co.uk/our-services/school-and-nursery-improvement-partner/psed

Erikson, E. (1950) *Childhood and Society.* New York: Norton.

Felitti, V., Anda, R., Nordenberg, D., Williamson, D. F., Spitz, A. M., Edwards, V., Koss, M. P. and Marks, J. S. (1998) "Relationship of Childhood Abuse and Household Dysfunction to Many of the Leading Causes of Death in Adults", *American Journal of Preventative Medicine,* 14(4), pp. 245–258.

Home Office (2015) *Controlling or Coercive Behaviour in an Intimate or Family Relationship: Statutory Guidance Framework.* London: Home Office. Available online: www.gov.uk/government/ publications/statutory-guidance-framework-controlling-or-coercive-behaviour-in-an-intimate-or-family-relationship

Howes N., "Here to Listen", in Howarth, J. (ed.) (2009) *The Child's World* (2nd edition), pp. 124–140. London: Jessica Kingsley.

Howes, N. (2014) A *Trauma Model for Planning, Assessing and Reviewing Contact for Looked-After Children.* London: Community Care Inform.

Humphreys, C. R., Mullender, A. and Skamballis, A. (2006) "'Talking to My Mum': Developing Communication Between Mothers and Children in the Aftermath of Domestic Violence", *Journal of Social Work*, 6(1), pp. 53–63. Available online: https://doi.org/10.1177/1468017306062223

James, B. (1994) *Handbook for Treatment of Attachment-Trauma Problems in Children.* New York: Free Press.

Katz, E. (2016a) *Coercive Control-Based Domestic Abuse: Impacts on Mothers and Children.* London, presentation, AVA (Against Violence and Abuse) training seminar, 28 January. Available online: https:// avaproject.org.uk/wp-content/uploads/2016/03/Emma-Katz-2016.pdf

Katz, E. (2016b) "Beyond the Physical Incident Model: How Children Living with Domestic Violence are Harmed by and Resist Regimes of Coercive Control", *Child Abuse Review*, 25(1), pp. 46–59.

Katz, E. (2019) "Coercive Control, Domestic Violence, and a Five-Factor Framework: Five Factors that Influence Closeness, Distance, and Strain in Mother–Child Relationships", *Violence Against Women*, 25(15), pp. 1829–1853. Available online: https://doi.org/10.1177/1077801218824998

McLaughlin, K. A., Sheridan, M. A. and Lambert, H. K. (2014) "Childhood Adversity and Neural Development: Deprivation and Threat as Distinct Dimensions of Early Experience", *Neuroscience & Biobehavioral Reviews*, 47, pp. 578–591. Available online: www.sciencedirect.com/science/article/pii/S0149763414002620

Mullender, A., Hague, G., Imam, U., Kelly, L., Malos, E. and Regan, L. (2002) *Children's Perspectives on Domestic Violence.* London: Sage.

Radford, L., Corral, S., Bradley, C., Fisher, H., Bassett, C., Howat, N. and Collinshaw, S. (2011) *Child Abuse and Neglect in the UK Today.* London: NSPCC.

SafeLives (2017) *Children's Insights National Dataset 2014–17: Specialist Children's Domestic Abuse Services.* Bristol: SafeLives. Available online: http://safelives.org.uk/sites/default/files/resources/Children%27s%20Insights%20dataset%202014-17%20v2.pdf

Appendix

Resolution or non-resolution of distress caused by a parent

Compare these two examples:

In a shopping centre a dad is walking with his three-year-old son, holding his hand and suddenly swinging him with one arm, catching him around the waist and throwing him in the air and catching him. The boy laughs, a gurgling infectious laugh which draws looks from other people around them. The dad notices his audience, puts his son down, nods to acknowledge his audience and throws the boy in the air again. Again, the child laughs but the laughter has an edge which gives the impression that what is happening is not quite right. Dad again smiles to his audience and again throws the child in the air. This time the child cries. Dad puts him down quickly, lowers his head and begins to walk away. The child reaches for his dad's hand. Dad pulls away and angrily tells the boy he is no fun, leaving him bereft.

In a busy shop a three-year-old who is trying to manage his growing distress is noticed. An adult goes towards him and asks if his mummy has lost him. He nods. The adult asks if she can help him find his mummy. He nods again and immediately takes the adult's hand. She wonders out loud what they could do to find his mummy. The suggestion that they shout for the boy's mummy is met with a mixture of a nod and a shake of his head. Noticing his confusion, she assures him by saying she will shout, not him. He nods. She asks what his mummy is called. He says, "Mummy". She says if she shouts "Mummy" all the mummies in the shop will answer, so she asks him what his daddy calls his mummy. He says, "Angela". She counts to three and shouts, "Angela". A man pushes through the crowd. The boy runs towards him shouting, "Daddy". They share the joy of their reunion and there are hugs and smiles. The dad says, "Sorry, so sorry we lost you", patting his son's back. The boy assures the dad he is OK and pats his dad's back reassuring his dad.

In the first example the child learns that taking care of an adult's needs is primary, don't expect care and comfort but take care of yourself. It is not just the event itself which causes the trauma but what was missing to assist in recovery or afterwards caused intense confusion when trying to make sense or what had just happened. Just like the child (Luna) in her bedroom who hears angry shouting and sounds of violence between the parents asks the next morning, "What happened last night?" and is told, "Nothing happened", or "Don't worry about it", or "It's OK it won't happen again", or "Your dad loves me, it was an accident", or "It was my fault", or "It was your fault because you . . .". The "window of tolerance" remains narrow.

Compare the impact on a healthy, happy teenager of being lost by a parent whilst shopping and how different this would be. The teenager may feel a bit of tolerable anxiety perhaps, even some annoyance or excitement, but can tell the difference between all these feelings. With a wider, age-appropriate window the teenager will have the ability to internally regulate or take care of themself. Compare the impact the experience would have on a teenager who has experienced persistent trauma and has a narrow window. This teenager feels intolerable anxiety, annoyance, abandonment, fear or excitement but cannot tell the difference between them, and now with a narrow, not age-appropriate window has limited ability to internally regulate or take care of themself and instead explodes with anger masking the other feelings – his anger is the answer but is seen by those around him as the problem.

How the brain and body respond to a challenge

Try this little exercise to help you understand and experience how your brain and body respond to a challenge. Notice while you do it if you are comfortable "in your window" with the three bits of your brain working together or whether you become uncomfortable and stop thinking and instead of solving the problem begin to deal with what you are feeling and how your body responds to these feelings. Notice how your thinking brain finds the answer to and solves the problem. Notice if you smile, laugh, wiggle, squiggle, bounce your knee, curl your toes, blink rapidly, feel smug, satisfied or silly. Notice the thoughts and feelings you have and how your body responds to these thoughts and feelings and work out whether the way your body responded to these was to do with solving this problem now or whether your responses came from another time when you had the same feelings.

On a piece of paper:

1. Write the letter V. Now add a line so that you are seeing the number 6.
2. Now write IX and add a line so that you are seeing the number 6.
3. Now write IX and add a line so that you are seeing the number 3.

Answers on page 45. (Notice when you decided to look at the answers. Think about whether that is what you usually do rather than persevering with puzzling for the answer when asked to do something. Notice your reaction to the answers and what thoughts come into your head, for example, "I was never good at maths", "That is so easy"," I could never have got that", "I'm so stupid". Whatever you tell yourself will be what you told yourself about yourself the first time, and many times afterwards, when you were experiencing these same feelings when you were near the edge of, or out of, your window.)

Using the paw prints or sticky notes to identify safe people/places

The purpose of using paw prints or sticky notes is to help the child and you identify who are the safe people and safe places for this particular child. This should be done in a playful way as if it is a game, albeit a serious game with an important purpose. It may surprise you who the child chooses – that is their choice and only if you know this is not a safe person would you gently disagree about their choice. The child might not choose the person or people you would expect them to. Again, that is their choice. It would be your judgement call about when, or maybe even if, you challenge this at the time or leave it till another time if you know this child is not at current risk from this person. Without blaming or shaming the child for their choice, have a conversation about what made them choose that person. It is important questions don't start with the word why. This is blaming and shaming and most likely to get the answer "I don't know" or silence or compliance and the search for what you want looked for rather than what the child is believing or thinking. Any question starting with why can instead be started with "Tell me what . . ." or "Describe to me what . . ." or "Explain to me what . . ." Doing this opens the conversation up rather than closing it down, enabling you to listen to and explore with the child who is a safe person or where is a safe place. It is not unusual for a child to want to stick the note for someone frightening on the back of the paper or even outside the room door and then shut the door on the note. Again, that is their choice.

The paw prints can be copied onto a sheet of paper. You can also cut them out and use them as if they were sticky notes. You will know the child you are going to do this with and how to word your questions to give the child the most help. Writing their answer or drawing a picture or sticking a sticky note to represent that person on each of the "toes".

Ideas on how to use this picture of Luna:

The child can doodle or colour in the picture.

The child can draw the feelings Luna might have in her tummy at different stages in her journey.

The picture could be used to create other situations or behaviours or endings for Luna .

How the brain and body respond to a challenge

Answers: 1) VI, 2) SIX and 3) Square root of IX (9) is 3 so a square root sign.